NEW BONUS CONTENT

WHY, WHEN & HOW

TO SELL

—— YOUR ——

RESTORATION BUSINESS

PROVEN STRATEGIES TO SECURE THE BEST OFFER

GOKUL PADMANABHAN

CONTENTS

INTRODUCTION

"The future has many names:

For the weak, it means the unattainable.

For the fearful, it means the unknown.

For the courageous, it means opportunity."

-Victor Hugo

One of the greatest lessons I've learned in over 15 years as a Restoration Specialist is the industry's sticking power. Restoration work is practically recession proof, and when the economy overshadows sales in other sectors, restoration businesses shine. Our industry is on a precipice, set to move forward in new and innovative ways based on the market today.

Yet even with its promising potential for growth, the reality of our industry is that 80% of all companies are unsellable. Add to this that 65% of current Restoration owners are baby boomers with 80% of their wealth locked in their business, and there are growing concerns over the health of restoration & remediation.

As the boomer population ages and moves toward retirement, it's important to bring positive solutions for creating a sellable business. To do this, we must take a hard look at the 20% of businesses in our industry that are sellable and determine what distinguishes them from the rest.

The solution to any problem begins with observation, and I've spent my 15 years speaking with over 1,000 business owners to find the magic of the 20% and learn what they do well. What I've discovered is a simple yet powerful formula that, when it's time for those owners to exit their businesses, brings great deals, multiple offers, and the exit they want based on the terms they set forth.

The Entrepreneur in Us All

I understand what it is to be an entrepreneur. I've included my personal business selling story as a part of this eBook, and I have learned a great deal about the ups and downs of entrepreneurship.

Let's face it, entrepreneurs are a wild bunch—a little crazy, with a sense of invincibility, and the tenacity and courage to take more risks for more reward. As entrepreneurs, we are forced to recognize the very real correlation between our risks and the desired outcomes. The entrepreneurial journey is never an easy one, but the lessons are like nothing else you'll experience in life—through the good times and bad.

Mastering the Game of Business

For some entrepreneurs, a business is just an asset or a tool. For others, it's their entire life. Some owners control their business, but some are left with an operation which consumes their time and talents, ultimately controlling them. Every business has the power to create or destroy, and it's clear that you must master the game of business, or the business will master you.

Are you Sellable or Unsellable?

A foundational understanding provides insight of what makes a business sellable and what keeps an owner stuck in an unsellable organization. It's important to evaluate where you and your business are today. Are you unsellable or on your way to the optimal business exit when the time comes?

THE 80-20 REALITY CHECK for Owners	
80% Unsellable Businesses - Owners are:	**20% Sellable Businesses - Owners are:**
Focused on daily operations	Focused on strategic objectives
Running the day-to-day business	Prepared with a plan and exit in mind
Focused on what's wrong	Focused on what's working
Stuck in the mindset of doing it themselves	Sticking with their core skills and building specialized teams
Focused on things they cannot control	Focused on things they can control
The center of all activities in the business	Able to remove themselves from the core business operations

WHY: Discovering the Why Behind Your Sale

"You must think about whether you're a really good shepherd of your company, your employees, and your customers."

– Gokul Padmanabhan

WHY DID YOU START A BUSINESS?

- I wanted to create FINANCIAL FREEDOM for myself and my family.
- I wanted to control my time.
- I desired a feeling of empowerment.
- I wanted security for my family.
- I wanted to help those I love and those in need.
- It's exciting.

Once you've discovered the why behind your startup, you can begin determining the why behind your new decision to sell.

Businesses mean very different things to different people. We often think a business is for life, but if you're working 12 hours a day, 7 days a week, are you really living into the reasons you started your business? Think back on your first day as a business owner. Was your goal to work 80 hours a week or make money and move on?

Businesses serve a purpose in your life. As with many things, sometimes it's very purposeful, and sometimes the purpose of it expires or runs out. I think part of being a successful entrepreneur is recognizing when you've peaked and when to exit a business—essentially when you are no longer the absolute best shepherd of your company. You've built your business, and you know it inside and out. Only you have the insight to determine what your best next step should be, with the help of some important questions to gauge your current state in your business and identify red flags.

Are you suffering from B.O.B.?

Business Owner Burnout is more than an acronym; it's a common phenomenon affecting small business owners, especially in the restoration industry. Running from job to job and managing employees takes its toll, and if you're not prepared for the gut punch of B.O.B., it'll consume you and hurt your business.

Does the following sound familiar? *You wake up in the morning dreading getting out of bed. It was a long night, and you just don't want to face another day. Worse still, it's Saturday, and your kids have a soccer game that you'll be missing again. You drag yourself out of bed, stop for that four-dollar cup of coffee, and head into the office. After three hours of paperwork, you drive to a job site to find your guys were late due to faulty equipment, and in the rush to make up the lost time, they've broken a customer's window. Here comes that extra insurance paperwork.*

BUSINESS OWNER BURNOUT IS ONE OF THE TOP REASONS SMALL BUSINESSES BEGIN TO FALTER AND EVENTUALLY FAIL.

Times like this are more than just a nightmare; they're a reality of business ownership. The demands are never ending, and you'll wake up the next day and face it all again.

When you're burned out and exhausted, your decision making is negatively affected, and that trickles down to negatively impact your employees, operations, and bottom line. When your relationships with employees, vendors, and customers suffer, the job you used to love becomes a frustrating burden. I speak from my own personal experience here, as well as that of hundreds of clients over the last fifteen years.

Acknowledging your burnout and making plans to move forward is the beginning of reversing the problem. Now, instead of dreading your day, you're prepping your business for sale, learning new things, and striving for achievable goals once more. The spring is back in your step, and your future excites you again.

DID YOU KNOW - Only Around 1% of Business Owners Have an Exit Plan in Place

Are you out of ideas and money to grow your market share?

New ideas are the lifeblood of small business growth, especially in an industry as crowded as restoration. When you first opened your doors, you were full of the life and verve that comes with a new endeavor. You were the idea master, and you actively engaged in your advertising, operations, innovations, and employee success.

Now you're noticing your market share is declining. Perhaps there's a newer, larger company moving into your territory. Maybe your market is saturated with smaller companies. Even if your profits hold steady, you may notice your business growth slowly shrinking. No longer are you on top of the pack, and your idea pool for regaining that market share is dwindling. You could purchase another business to acquire that larger market share, but the will and the capital is lacking.

The desire to hang on while profits hold steady is strong, and you're convinced you'll recover. This is just a bump in the road, right? The evidence begins to support the time to sell, but you also have a desire to wade through and keep on pushing. Perhaps, it's best to cash in before the market—and your energy—erodes further.

Are you being a good shepherd for your employees & customers?

Is it getting more and more difficult to keep up with technology?

To stay competitive in your business, you need to be on top technologically. The growth touted by your competition may make their offerings seem sweeter, and to maintain your edge, you'll need to keep up with each advancement.

You continue to invest in the latest equipment and education for your employees, but you're left with outdated machinery, and you may even be making payments on the outmoded technology, even as you acquire the newest and best. The constant cycle of recycling the used while investing in the new is critical to success, and if you find yourself unable to keep up, your cashflow will take a negative hit.

Who would take over your business?

Closing up shop and retiring is not an option. You've got employees to look after, and just leaving means abandoning money on the table. You need to place someone in your position, but you may not have a qualified person at the ready. Maybe there are a few viable candidates, but none of them can raise the capital to buy you out.

88% of business owners believe someone in their family will run their small business within five years, yet only 30% of small businesses extend to the second generation, and just 3% operate into the third.

Your next move cannot rely on a dream that has proven false for so many. While the idea of selling may seem daunting, developing a succession plan is critical.

ASK YOURSELF - Are you the bottle neck for growth?

Other Signs That It Is *Time to Sell*

Your top manager is retiring or leaving to pursue other opportunities, and you have no replacement prospect waiting in the wings. Your employees are assets and contribute value to your business. Sell before your sale price is affected by the departure of a key player.

Running a business is taxing to your health. If your business operation is degrading your wellbeing, you are putting yourself and your family at risk.

Your family business is causing internal conflict. Life is too short to let your business create a rift between you and your family members.

Your family no longer knows you. Your partner no longer knows the sound of your voice, and the dog goes bonkers when you pull in the driveway. If your business has separated you from your family, you risk damaging the most vital part of your life.

Understanding the whys of selling your restoration business is the first step in determining if the time is right for you.

CONSIDER THIS - Businesses fail every 9-10 years.

Most people think businesses are for life, but businesses fail every nine to ten years. When I say this, people raise their eyebrows, but when a business hits year eight, it's a safe bet that change is coming. Every nine to ten years, everything about your business changes, and unless you're willing to shepherd it through this flux and into a new era, you need to recognize that it's ok to get out.

Ask yourself these questions to determine if it may be time to sell:

- ✓ Am I satisfied with my day-to-day happiness level owning this business?
- ✓ Am I less motivated than I once was and becoming a bottleneck for my business?
- ✓ How are my energy levels each day as I go to work?
- ✓ Do I have a desire to come into work and fight every single day to keep the business healthy and growing?
- ✓ Do I still enjoy running teams and managing people?
- ✓ Are there any players in the market who are posing a threat to our market share or more risk to our operations?

WHEN: Identifying the Optimal Time to Sell

"In the business world, the rearview mirror is always clearer than the windshield."

– Warren Buffet

Don't Wait Too Long

A few years ago, I met with a Florida restoration business owner in his early sixties. His business revenue was well over $4 Million, and he had an impressive 7,000 sq. ft. facility. I estimated a sale for $2.7 million on the open market if he sold at that peak, as he was nearing retirement.

He politely declined and assured me his business would continue to grow for a few more years, but sadly, he was mistaken.

The business environment began its natural decline, and his profits quickly eroded. He laid off many loyal employees and he worked 80+ hours a week to stay afloat. Three years later, when we met again, I had the unfortunate task of informing him his business was essentially unsellable.

He had to close his doors, lay off the rest of his workforce, and sell his equipment for a mere $450,000. His entire life's work netted him just 16% of what he could have made only a few years earlier.

Missing the boat on selling high was more than just an unfortunate turn; It was a devastating reduction in circumstances at the retirement stage of his life and the sad end of his beloved business venture.

Could you be moving toward making the same mistake?

Stages of Business

You've heard it before: buy low; sell high. It sounds simple enough, but this key principle has funneled the nation's wealth into 10% of the population.

But what about you? You have been in the business a long time, so you have a good sense about what's happening around you. Still, it takes intensive market research to determine the best time to sell a business.

Startup Stage – A small business in the startup stage is highly dependent on the owner's ability to realize his vision. The business is an unknown quantity, and buyers are generally uninterested in purchasing.

Early Growth Stage – Buyer interest emerges as the business begins breaking even and continuing to grow. While not a prime candidate for purchase, certain strategic buyers may consider acquiring the business and adding their own product or new revenue channels.

Accelerated Development Stage – The company is in its prime for potential buyers as the business faces dramatic increases in sales and profits. The working capital and credit are nearly maxed, and the business is beginning to grow beyond current management.

Maturity Stage – As your company settles into its niche, sales and profits begin to level off or erode slightly. The continued competition is fierce, and your business may struggle to maintain its foothold in the marketplace. Mature businesses remain attractive when their track record is primarily positive.

Declining Stage – A business seeing a sustained erosion in profits and facing intense competition may have a hard time holding onto personnel. These business types may attract *Turnaround Specialists* who can provide capital to prop up the business. These buyers are rare, highly specialized, and offer lower prices.

The stages of business development are not always linear. Your business may cycle through stages two, three, and four several times over. Businesses become most attractive to buyers when they are in an accelerated growth stage and their profit projections are high.

The window for prime selling is often missed for emotional reasons. No one wants to sell when they're turning a hefty profit, but booming businesses command the best possible price.

I've Been There

Let me speak frankly, business owner to business owner. I know where you are because I've been there. In addition to spending 15 years helping business owners in the restoration space, I've also been the seller in my own business transaction. I've made mistakes, done the legwork, and experienced the emotions that follow sellers along the path to exiting their business. Your personal experience is important, but your buyer will be looking at the transaction from a more practical, asset-centric lens.

The Cold Hard Facts and Inarguable Truths That Run Counter to Our Human Psychology & Attachments

Your business is nothing more than an asset that is producing a reasonable cash flow for the time you've invested.

✓ Buyers view assets as items, not as emotional attachments with meaning outside of their value.
✓ Assets often lose value due to unforeseen circumstances. The smart solution is buying a business at wholesale and selling for retail.
✓ When you become attached, selling when it's financially smart will be a difficult challenge to overcome.

OK—so you've made your decision to plan an exit strategy, now it's time to go do it.

HOW: Increasing Value Through 6 Success Drivers

When a reporter asked John D. Rockefeller, "How much money is enough?"

He responded, "Just a little bit more."

Just as running a successful company has its own strategies and technologies, exiting a company and preparing it for sale requires its own unique playbook and set of actions. These two business operation focuses are completely different—if you continue to run your business in operations mode while trying to sell it, you're leaving a lot of money on the table.

Any sports strategy consists of very different approaches to offense and defense, and exiting your business is much the same. Your approach must change to affect the desired outcome. The best way to move forward is to learn from those who have mastered the game.

Tony Robbins tells us that success leaves clues. I've spent years studying the clues and considering how the successful sellers bring their businesses to close with an optimal offer. I work with my clients go out and do the same. Whether your company is big or small, six master plays will create a sellable business. It's time to roll up your sleeves and get to it.

1: Master Your Business Finances

There are many factors that buyers consider when purchasing a business, and financial strength often makes up the largest part of the consideration criteria. When buyers are looking at your business, the only way they're going to know how well your business is doing is to review all of your financial documents. You must these documents in order, following standard accounting principles, so you can clearly show a buyer the true performance of the business and attract better offers.

If buyers believe they'll need to inject cash into a business after purchase, they're going to discount their offer. They may even walk away entirely. Good books, both cash and accrual, are a gamechanger. Your prospective buyers will review five years of financials, and it's important to have your books aligned.

Take time to analyze your cashflow and understand obstacles. You may be surprised by the number of self-inflicted challenges and the easy solutions to overcome them. Tighten up efficiency and work as effectively as possible to reduce costs and invest in better customer billing practices. Keep in mind, revenue and profitability trends matter.

Accounting and financial statements are the language of business. This unique language is how we communicate to a buyer the reason they should consider your business. Some of the financial documents a buyer is going to look for include the following:

- 5 years of tax returns
- 5 years of accrual profit & loss and balance sheets
- 5 years of cash profit & loss and balance sheets
- WIP report
- Accounts receivable report
- Accounts payable report

In my opinion, this is the number one reason companies don't sell. They just cannot produce standard financial reports and clearly articulate financial performance to the buyer.

Financial Check-In:

- Am I artificially reducing profits by expensing personal items?
- Is my bookkeeping professional?
- Am I running the business lean?

2: Master Growth Potential

Buyers will pay more for a business that is growing or has evidence-based growth potential. They want to see themselves successful in the business. If a business is declining or stagnant, they will pay less. If you're selling your business as it's growing, you'll get top dollar.

Every business goes through stages of growth. It's counterintuitive that you want to sell a business when it's growing fast, not when it's declining. When we present a growing business to a buyer and show them a path to even greater profitability, the business is worth exponentially more than when it is declining.

Most entrepreneurs have a tendency to hold onto their business longer than they should, thus hurting themselves trying to sell at the wrong time. Most people call me when they're in decline and they want to be rid of their problem.

Growth Potential Check-In:

- Has my business reached its fullest growth potential?
- Am I doing everything I can to continue growing my business?
- Can I expand my services?
- If I had a check for $100,000, how would I use it to grow the company?

3: Master Revenue & Customer Diversity

Buyers will pay a lot of money for a business if they can be reasonably confident that the business is going to produce dependable revenue over time.

Buyers are wary of business owners who put all eggs in one basket. If your customer base consists of one or two large clients, buyers see signs of instability. Diversifying takes many shapes and forms to bring your current products and services to new markets.

Losing that high-volume customer could put the business in jeopardy. Consider diversifying your suppliers as well as your clients to find new revenue potential and stability.

Never allow more than 20% of your revenue to be sourced by one client or third-party administrator.

Diversifying Check In:

- Rate your customers from smallest to largest. What can you do to increase business with your smaller customers?
- Rate your customers from easiest to most difficult to replace. What can you do to become less dependent on those most difficult to replace?

4: Master Developing and Documenting Your Sales & Marketing

Every buyer is going to ask, *"How will the revenue and sales continue when I buy the business?"* Beyond financial performance, knowing how you generate new business, and the sequencing of your marketing process creates value to your operations.

Document your sales and marketing procedures to help your potential buyers envision the profitability and growth potential of your business.

Documenting and maintaining successful sales and marketing strategies—that can be duplicated without you in the business—vastly increases the value of your company in the eyes of a buyer. A buyer wants to know what works so they can easily replicate your operations once they take control.

New buyers need to know that your business-building and customer relationship strategies are transferable.

Sales & Marketing Check In:

- Do you have a documented marketing plan?
- Do you have a list of customer names or a database?
- Can you explain to a buyer how you generate business?

5: Master Building a Positive Reputation

Knowing what percentage of your circle would recommend you to a colleague or friend creates a marketing foundation and competitive edge.

Understanding how likely your clients, supporters, and general network would be to recommend you to others is a powerful metric. The *Net Promoter Score* (NPS) methodology is a simple and effective way to determine—with one question—whether your company is holding its own in the marketplace.

Your success lies in your reputation and the likelihood of your past clients and current business partners to promote you. Your NPS is not only a predictor of success, but it often speaks to how well you're managing the other five master plays discussed on these pages. Establishing quality systems, marketing, and teams directly correlates with client experience and your reputation in the industry.

The ability to measure customer satisfaction and visualize how your business measures up is of utmost importance to prospective buyers.

Reputation Check In:

- Do you know your Net Promoter Score and how to leverage this information to better your business and reputation?
- Do you have methods to measure customer satisfaction?
- Do you monitor what your customers are saying about your company online?

6: Master Building Your Bench Strength & Management Team

When companies are looking at your business, having a strong, capable management team that can run day-to-day operations after the transition is over is invaluable. Buyers want to know that your business is sustainable and profitable once you are removed from the equation. Creating employees and customers who are loyal to your brand—not just loyal to you—can sustain profitability upon your departure.

Begin removing yourself gradually from the day-to-day operations. Empower your managers to make key decisions so they have the skillset to run the business in your post-closing absence. Identify who has the capacity to fulfill your duties and begin training them in key components of the business.

A strategic succession plan ensures that you have the right people in place to drive business once you're gone.

Buyers will look closely at your management team and assess your staff performance when preparing their offer price. A quality management team will invite a new buyer into a seamless transition with little disruption to business operations.

If a buyer suspects customers and employees will walk if you leave, they will heavily discount their offering price or make no offer at all.

Bench Strength Check In:

- Track a "day in the life" for you in your business. What observations can you make?
- Are there current employees that can expand their role in the business?
- Do your customers require that <u>you</u> serve them instead of letting your staff handle their needs?

Increasing the value of your business and preparing to sell are not mutually exclusive goals. Increasing your business value is inherently positive and puts you in the position to sell when you're ready.

CONCLUSION

"There is only one way to avoid criticism: Do nothing. Say nothing. Be nothing."

-Aristotle

Selling your restoration business is an important and weighty decision, and you have limited opportunity to get it right and sell on your terms. The selling process can take as long as two years and is extremely complicated. If you don't anticipate the pitfalls, you'll find yourself making costly errors and devaluing your business.

- Sound financials are not just about having financial stability in your business but about being able to prove your financial status through proper bookkeeping and documentation.
- Don't be afraid to begin the selling process while the business is in growth mode. Success lies in showing the potential for future scaling in the business.
- Pursue diverse revenue streams to protect your business when a client leaves or a revenue stream becomes less lucrative. Your diverse revenue safeguards you from dependence on one key client.
- Understand the power of your marketing plan and put it in writing. Buyers want to see how you reach customers and be assured that you have systems and processes in place for continued growth.
- Loyal customers and a large client network are a win when proving your worth. Your best marketing comes from satisfied customers and business partners.
- A high-value workforce, such as skilled technicians and experienced managers, increases your business value in the eyes of a buyer.

If you're planning to tackle the sale of your business independently, ask yourself these questions:

- Can I accurately evaluate my business and develop an appropriate asking price?
- Do I have experience in analyzing recent sales in the restoration business sales market?
- Do I know how to position my business for sale in a way that appropriately generates competitive offers from qualified buyers?
- Do I have experience negotiating a selling price?

If you can't confidently answer yes to all of these questions, seek the assistance and support of a professional. Restoration Brokers of America works with businesses like yours to evaluate the pitfalls of selling and answer these tough questions about creating a solid exit strategy. As specialists in the restoration space, our experience becomes your leg up in a competitive market.

ABOUT RESTORATION BROKERS OF AMERICA

Restoration Brokers of America was built to serve sellers in the restoration space and help them identify the factors that bring success in a sales transaction. We are restoration specialists with over $500 Million in restoration company sales, and over 95% of our clients get their businesses sold.

Our goal at RBA is to create maximum sales prices for your company by implementing our proven drivers for business success. We market your business to over 900 qualified buyers to create demand for your business. With our proven restoration business practices, we help business owners determine next steps, whether your business is in the selling stage or not.

With over 15 years specializing in the sale of restoration businesses, we build relationships with straightforward advice and proven practices to maximize your selling price and exposure to qualified buyers—closing more sales than anyone in the restoration industry.

SELLER STORIES

The best advice comes from experience, and I have been honored to walk through transactions with business owners who understand how to leverage their successes and create optimal business transactions for the buyer and the seller.

We've collected stories from our clients and found them so compelling that we chose to share one as a bonus. The second seller story is an account of my own experience selling a business that was outside of the restoration space and the cycle of emotions and events that I experienced. These stories provide an account of the selling experience, outlining the process, emotions and advice to support future sellers.

Third Time's a Charm

SCOTT MILLER - *Business coach and former restoration company owner with experience owning and operating multiple businesses, in and outside of the restoration space.*

I've been in the restoration industry since 2005—started as a franchisee and later became an independent. I sold my business in 2017. When I started my restoration business, I got a business coach a few months in and loved that I had someone who was bringing accountability to me. I was Rookie of the Year in the franchise system, and a lot of folks reached out to ask me what I was doing, which is how I transitioned into business coaching in 2008.

I always had a really systematic approach to the business, and the driver for me was to get the business in good shape, document systems, and delegate a backup for every position.

What drove that for me was not initially selling, but to create time so I could do what I really loved. I remember coming home and telling my wife about the highlight of my day, which was getting a phone call from someone to help.

It wasn't part of the plan from the start to sell my business. Jokingly, I say I first thought about it the first time I found myself in a basement removing sewage water, but I had thought about it over the years and started the process a few times before I ultimately sold. I didn't start the business thinking specifically about when I would sell.

After almost thirteen years of being in the business, the 24/7 nature of the work was hanging over my head, and I had the business coaching which I loved. When I found Gokul, he was certain he had buyers in line, and I was convicted that this was finally the right time to sell.

It was the perfect time for me—the business was in the best shape it had ever been in, and we used a book, *Traction,* by Gene L. Wickman to get the business where it needed to be. I felt like revenue and profitability were really strong, and the team was in really good shape. I loved what I was doing and wanted to do more of it. I took a leap and thought, "let's try this." If it didn't happen, it would have been ok, but it happened very quickly.

Within two weeks of listing the business I had two buyers, and it was important that I felt comfortable that whoever bought would keep the team in place and interact well. I wanted the person who had the best chance of success. Business partners from outside our geographic area wanted to expand into our market, and after meeting with them, it felt right. The offers were similar, and I knew one was a better fit.

Leading up to closing day was an emotional roller coaster. The closing went smoothly, and the biggest thing hanging over my head was letting people know. That day, I met with one person face-to-face and then started calling on others to let them know, one-on-one. I did not enjoy keeping the secret, but it was necessary. Gokul explained to me, even up to the closing table, sometimes deals fall apart, and it was vital to maintain confidentiality until we were closed, but that was the toughest part for me.

Every once in a while, I miss the excitement and comradery of the restoration business, but now I'm an extension of those teams through consulting. I always look back fondly on the very unique restoration experiences—the surge events and comradery in the office as we'd answer emergency calls. My old business is still going strong with quite a few of the key employees still working under new ownership.

A lot of my consulting clients are being approached about selling in this unique landscape. There's a lot in the due diligence phase, and the value of your business is really a function of what they're able to take out of the business. My advice?

- Really evaluate and have a strong understanding of your financials.
- Get a sense of where you are on the spectrum in terms of profitability in the industry. If you're going to sell, it's important to maximize what you're getting for the business.
- If you're not in tune with your financials, step one is getting there and understanding what you as the owner can take from the business.
- If you're not, find a professional to help you understand your profitability in the business, then strategize on how to become more profitable if you're not as profitable as the industry standard.

Next, become as insignificant to the business as you can. A buyer wants to buy your team, not the owner. While there are some exceptions for large acquisition firms or aggregators who want the owner to stay on, for the most part having an owner who is not integral is important. In my case, I was not going on jobs and the contacts were not directly tied to me. Everything was happening in the business without me, which was critical.

It's really important to find someone who understands our industry. Don't try to go it alone even though it's attractive. My first attempt was a local broker. I did not realize there was someone in the industry who specialized, so I chose someone local who sold every sort of business but knew the area. He had the listing agreement for a year and there was no activity. I then started telling people in the community that I might sell. That process took about 18 months. Since I was going it alone, I wasted a lot of time, but I found Gokul and sold the business. It took almost a year, but he found the buyer in two weeks. It's really important that you get someone who is well connected throughout this unique industry and avoid going it alone.

Selling My OWN Business Was Hard—and I'm a Broker!

The 7 Emotions of Selling

GOKUL PADMANABHAN – *Owner & CEO of Restoration Brokers of America with experience owning and operating multiple businesses.*

Business mergers and acquisitions have been my strength, passion and daily profession for 15 years. I serve my clients by preparing and marketing their businesses to the best buyers. I walk them through the offer-to-close process with confidence and security. I enjoy, more than almost anything, moving a business through sale to a smooth and satisfying conclusion for the buyer and the seller. I've built my company and reputation on specializing in the restoration industry.

But in 2021, I found myself on the other side of the process—preparing to sell a business I owned outside of restoration and remediation. What I learned about the process and myself was eye-opening for me as an agent. What a game changer it was experiencing what I now call, *The Seven Emotions of a Business Sale.*

THE SEVEN EMOTIONS OF A BUSINESS SALE

Emotion 1: Guilt – The Listing Process

You may think about selling for years, but it's not real until you take those first steps. For me, I'd thought about selling for over two years before I hired an agent. Until that point, it was a dream, a window-shopping experience, a what-if. And, even when it was time to get the valuation on the business, it was still not real, just an exercise.

It became real when I signed the initial listing and engagement agreement. I felt like I was cheating on the employees and letting them down. With one signature, I moved from that surreal dreaming space to extreme guilt.

It helped me to keep focused on my long-term life strategy. This business was not serving me well, and the employees needed someone who was more motivated and focused on running and growing it. With that thought in mind, I was able to move through that first stage of guilt.

Emotion 2: You've GOT to be Kidding – Buyer Questions

We listed the business, and the broker sent me confidentiality agreements. My first call with the buyer was really interesting. I had to explain the reasons why I bought the business in the first place. It took me back to when the business was more important to me, when I was more motivated and active. I had a bit of seller's remorse, and I could hear my inner monologue accusingly whisper, "If it's so good, why are you selling it?"

After the first meeting, we did a showing at the office, and the questions from the buyer got detailed and very deep. They asked me why I did certain things, and I found myself getting short-tempered and snippy because I wasn't used to answering questions from people about my practices. I told my wife, "I know I need an attitude adjustment. I know the buyer is just asking me questions in earnest, and I need to calm down and really explain to him why I do certain things." After that attitude adjustment, it got better and progressed smoothly.

Emotion 3: Uncertainty – The Offer

The very first buyer gave us an offer. We were lucky in that respect. As much as I do this every day, when the broker called and let me know we were expecting an offer, I grew anxious. I did my best not to think about it too much during the day and lower my expectations. I assumed it wasn't going to be a good offer, but when I received the offer, there were a lot of good points and only one or two that I did not like. I reminded myself it was never going to be perfect, and I had to put on my agent hat and give myself a talk. "Gokul, if you've got the most important aspects, you should consider moving forward."

I slept on it and had a much-needed adjustment and recalibration. The offer had six of the ten most important things to me, and I decided to counter, which was accepted. Despite my experience in helping others navigate the very same process, I had to continue reminding myself that, with every offer, there are always going to be aspects that don't suit the seller's exact wishes.

Emotion 4: Pain Like a Root Canal – Due Diligence

With the offer step complete, we went on to due diligence when we really opened up our company so the buyer could ensure he was buying what was advertised. This felt like nothing short of a root canal as I provided everything about our business from the past five years. It was a lot of work collecting financials and all of the documents the buyer requested. One of the things we did well was, instead of dragging this on for weeks and weeks, I went to the office on a Saturday and just collected everything in one day. I didn't want to put myself through prolonged pain.

It took the buyer about three weeks to finish due diligence and get the bank financing ready. At this point it was difficult going to the office knowing this deal was progressing and becoming more certain. I had to maintain the confidentiality and keep reminding myself why I was selling the business in the first place.

Emotion 5: Where Are the Rainbows & Unicorns?? – The Closing

Going into closing, it was really interesting to be on the other side of the table as a seller. The morning of closing was exciting and nerve wracking at the same time. It was uneventful and took 20 minutes to sign papers and receive all financing and bank documents.

Once signed, the attorney said, "Well, you're done. Congratulations." I was numb. I thought I'd be excited. Where were the rainbows and unicorns? Instead, my attention immediately turned to how to train the buyer for success during our transition period. I thought I'd be over the moon and ready to celebrate, but after a quick meeting in the attorney's office, it was just done and over. Everything signed. Congrats - that's it.

Emotion 6: Sleepless Night – Informing the Team

I don't think I slept a wink the night before I had to tell the employees I'd sold the business. Lots of questions swirled in my head. Would they be mad at me? Would there be a sense of betrayal? Would they feel like I let them down? I didn't want my employees to feel like they were inadequate or the reason I sold the business. I wondered how they would take to the new owner. Would the key people stay? How could I make the reveal and transition the most positive experience possible?

My reaction surprised me. I regularly coach my clients to make this transition to new ownership, but when it was my turn, the feeling was unexpectedly heavy. On the Monday morning following the closing, I gathered the leadership first, and it was every bit as intense as I thought it would be. I then spoke with the rest of the group and introduced them to the new owner later that afternoon. There were tears and big emotions and those who expressed they were sad to see me go.

I stepped back and let the new owner lead the conversation. When he started talking about his vision and how he wanted to grow the company, the staff was more receptive than I could have hoped. It was clear that many were open to new leadership on the team, and they were excited.

I chose a Monday to make my announcement because I wanted the employees to become used to the new owner without the weekend to overthink and let their minds go to dark places. Looking back, maybe I assigned too much importance to my role in the business. The team was able to successfully move on with the new owner. No one quit, and there were no big upsets. The new owner led the charge, and the business moved on. Much of my concern was based on the misconception that the business could not run without me.

Emotion 7: Reality & Relief – The Transition

After the closing and announcement to the staff, I jumped immediately into training the new buyer, and I went above and beyond to set up the new owner for success. The two weeks after closing were extremely busy as I supported the buyer and asked myself, "What else can I teach him?"

During that time, I was still at the office early every day to see the employees and help with operations. For two weeks, it was as if nothing had changed. It wasn't until training had completed that I woke up on a Monday morning and realized I didn't need to go back to the office. The employees weren't waiting for me, and my phone was oddly silent. As I sat drinking my coffee, the emotion of the journey washed over me culminating in complete relief. I looked around me and was genuinely glad I'd sold my business.

My experience with the sale of a business has been an eye opening one, and it's helped me realize the full spectrum of emotion my clients encounter during the selling process. I've learned each step of the way, and what I used to believe about selling a business has been refocused to include the emotional journey my sellers experience. Understanding the steps to selling your business is important in an agent, but my own selling experience has enriched my understanding, and I'm more excited than ever to walk alongside you as you navigate the highs, lows, and in-betweens of selling your restoration business.

FINAL THOUGHTS

Why, When & How to Sell Your Restoration Business is an educational pillar in Restoration Brokers of America's unique strategy for bringing sellers to a successful business sale. Planning the best exit from a business is difficult and requires more than a quick and desperate decision based on extenuating circumstances.

I believe firmly in the power of education, and I have built the RBA Team to approach each unique challenge with laser focus and specialty advice. I'm most proud of the ways in which Restoration Brokers of America has grown to do more than sell businesses. We educate and advise our clients on the best ways to strengthen their selling potential. Before we sell, we coach, and for those businesses that are unsellable, we work hard to help change that business trajectory and prepare for the best possible sale at the right time, to the right buyer, and with the leverage that comes from proper planning.

No matter the stage of your business, looking forward to a future exit that has been properly planned and executed is important. If you have questions about the current state of your business, the RBA Team is ready to listen. Together, we'll sit down and confidentially review your business specifics and determine the best path forward for you.

RESTORATION BROKERS OF AMERICA

Restoration Brokers of America
www.RBASells.com
407-781-4596
info@RBASells.com

www.ingramcontent.com/pod-product-compliance
Lightning Source LLC
Chambersburg PA
CBHW011200220326
41597CB00026BA/4699